MY FIRST

PHOTOGRAPHY
B·O·O·K

DAVE KING

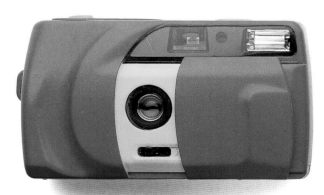

DK

DORLING KINDERSLEY
London • New York • Stuttgart

A Dorling Kindersley Book

For June, Lawrence, Sam, and Barney

Art Editor Mandy Earey
Project Editor Dawn Sirett
Production Louise Barratt
Managing Editor Jane Yorke
Managing Art Editor Gillian Allan

Photography Dave King

Additional photographs
Gillian Allan (best friends p.14), Jeremy Evans (two cars in photo album p.3 and p.41) Pete Gardner (animals p.15), David Horne (blurred party p.2 and p.14), Jane Horne (sand dunes p.2 and pp.16-17), June King (viewpoints p.2 and p.15, and children in picture frame and flowers in picture frame p.3 and p.39), Stella Love (elephant pp.32-33) and Martin Wilson (in and out of focus p.14 and car wheel p.3 and pp.41-42).

First published in Great Britain in 1994
by Dorling Kindersley Limited,
9 Henrietta Street, London WC2E 8PS

Copyright © 1994 Dorling Kindersley Limited, London

A CIP catalogue record for this book is available from the British Library.

ISBN 0-7513-5206-3

Colour reproduction by Colourscan, Singapore
Printed and bound in Italy by L.E.G.O.

Dorling Kindersley would like to thank the following for their help in producing this book: Mark Richards for jacket design, Jack Challoner, Jonathan Buckley, Chris Scollen, and Helen Drew. Dorling Kindersley would also like to give special thanks to the following for appearing in this book: Victoria Chandler, Ebru Djemal, Josey Edwards, Arran Hall, Daniel Lawrence, Jonathan Lawrence, Keat Ng, Jade Ogugua, Tebedge Ricketts, and Stacie Terry.

Illustrations by Coral Mula and Adrienne Hutchinson

CONTENTS

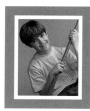  

PHOTOGRAPHY BY PICTURES

My First Photography Book shows you how to take creative pictures with a simple fixed focus or disposable camera. You will also find lots of fun projects to make with your photographs. On the opposite page is a list of things to remember when using this book, and below are the points to look for on each page. Photography words and terms are explained on page 48.

How to use this book

The things you need
The things to collect for each project are shown life-size to help you check that you have everything you will need.

Equipment
Illustrated checklists show you which tools you will need to have ready before you start each project.

Step-by-step
Step-by-step photographs and clear instructions tell you exactly what to do at each stage of a project.

MAKE IT MOVE!
When you look at a sequence of action photographs passing quickly before your eyes, the images look as if they are moving, just like a film at the cinema. You can see this effect by looking into a machine called a zoetrope. Before you make the zoetrope, you will need to take 13 photographs showing someone doing each stage of a simple action. Below, photographs of a clown lifting his hat and then putting it back on are used.

You will need

Coloured card

A sequence of 13 action photographs taken on a plain background

Jar lid

Two empty cotton reels

Coloured sticky tape

Medium-sized beads

Strong glue   Pencil

EQUIPMENT
Scissors
Compass
Pencil
Craft knife
Ruler

Making the zoetrope

1 Use a compass to draw a circle with a radius of 12.5 cm on card. Cut it out. Draw round a cotton reel in the circle's centre.

2 Ask an adult to cut slightly within the cotton reel circle, making a hole that the cotton reel fits into without sliding out.

3 Glue one cotton reel on to the inside of a jar lid and one to the outside. Glue a pencil into the reel on the outside of the lid.

4 Cut a strip of card 11.5 cm x 81 cm*. Measure 0.5 cm wide slots every 5.5 cm. Mark them all along one edge of the card.

5 Mark each of the 0.5 cm wide slots to be 4 cm deep. Use a ruler to draw the slots neatly. Cut them out.

6 Overlap the ends of the slotted card and glue them to make a tube. Tape the circle of card to the tube to make a base.

7 Trim the prints to make small rectangles and stick them on to a strip of card 7.5 cm x 80 cm**. Leave a 2 cm gap at one end.

8 Overlap the card by 2 cm and glue it to make a tube with the prints on the inside. Put the card in the drum, and beads in the jar lid.

9 Push the cotton reel through the hole in the base of the drum. It should fit snugly. The zoetrope is now ready to spin!

*You can stick two strips of card together to make it stronger. We have used yellow and blue card.

**The cut-out prints should measure 6 cm x 6 cm. Stick them down in order to make an action sequence.

44

45

Things to remember

1 Read all the instructions and gather together everything you will need before you begin a project.

2 Hold your camera still when you take a photograph.

3 Read the instructions that come with your camera so that you know how to use and look after it.

4 Use your camera's flash when taking photographs indoors or in poor light.

5 Be very careful when using scissors or sharp knives. **Do not use them unless an adult is there to help you.**

6 Wear an apron when using paint or glue and tidy up when you have finished.

What the page is about
The introduction to each page tells you important information about the activity shown.

The finished project
Life-size photographs show you what the finished projects look like, helping you to make them.

"How to use" instructions
Look out for these special boxes at the end of a project that show you how to use what you have made.

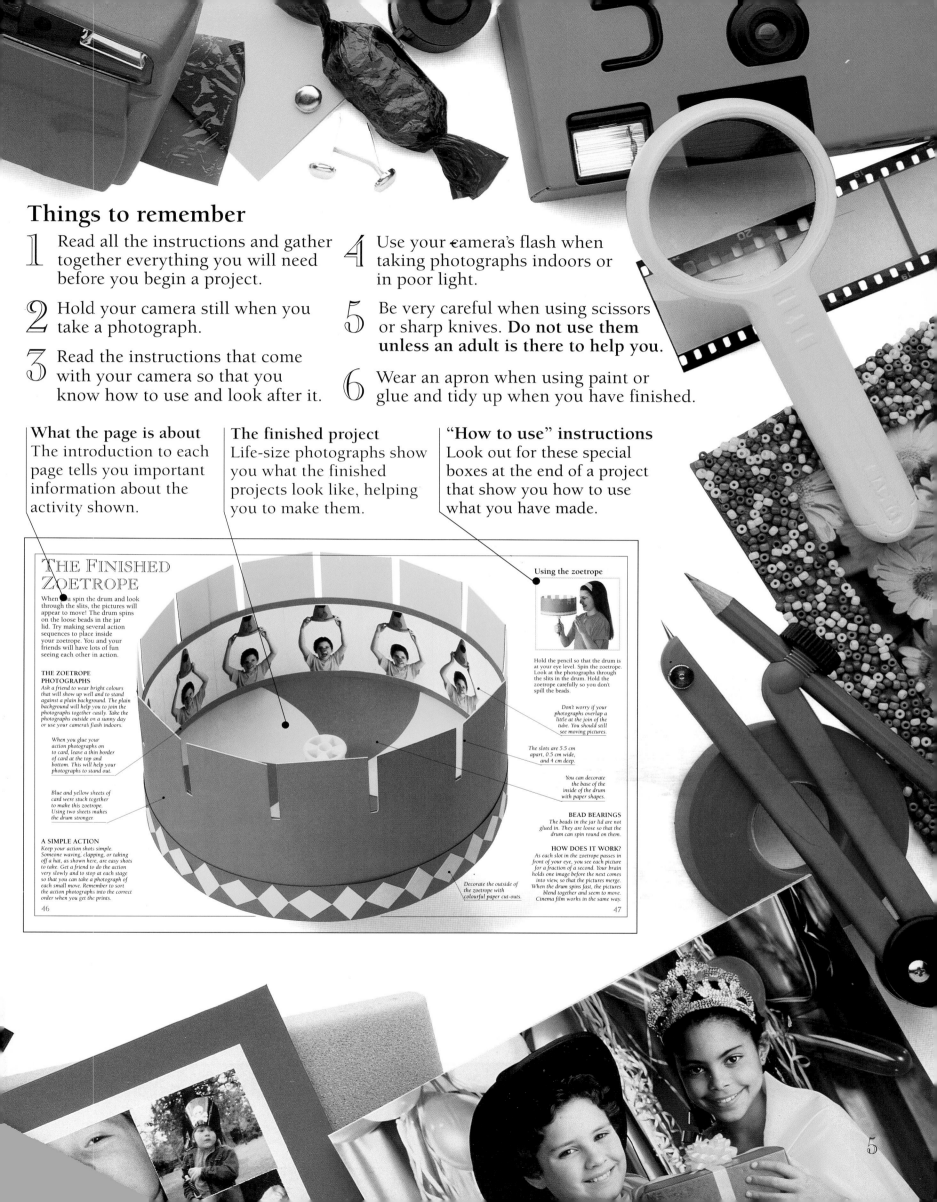

THE FINISHED ZOETROPE

When you spin the drum and look through the slits, the pictures will appear to move! The drum spins on the loose beads in the jar lid. Try making several action sequences to place inside your zoetrope. You and your friends will have lots of fun seeing each other in action.

THE ZOETROPE PHOTOGRAPHS
Ask a friend to wear bright colours that will show up well and to stand against a plain background. The plain background will help you to join the photographs together easily. Take the photographs outside on a sunny day or use your camera's flash indoors.

When you glue your action photographs on to card, leave a thin border of card at the top and bottom. This will help your photographs to stand out.

Blue and yellow sheets of card were stuck together to make this zoetrope. Using two sheets makes the drum stronger.

A SIMPLE ACTION
Keep your action shots simple. Someone waving, clapping, or taking off a hat, as shown here, are easy shots to take. Get a friend to do the action very slowly and to stop at each stage so that you can take a photograph of each small move. Remember to sort the action photographs into the correct order when you get the prints.

Decorate the outside of the zoetrope with colourful paper cut-outs.

Using the zoetrope

Hold the pencil so that the drum is at your eye level. Spin the zoetrope. Look at the photographs through the slits in the drum. Hold the zoetrope carefully so you don't spill the beads.

Don't worry if your photographs overlap a little at the join of the tube. You should still see moving pictures.

The slots are 5.5 cm apart, 0.5 cm wide, and 4 cm deep.

You can decorate the base of the inside of the drum with paper shapes.

BEAD BEARINGS
The beads in the jar lid are not glued in. They are loose so that the drum can spin round on them.

HOW DOES IT WORK?
As each slot in the zoetrope passes in front of your eye, you see each picture for a fraction of a second. Your brain holds one image before the next comes into view, so that the pictures merge. When the drum spins fast, the pictures blend together and seem to move. Cinema film works in the same way.

46

47

PINHOLE CAMERA

Make a pinhole in a light-proof box, put tracing paper on the opposite side, and instantly you have a simple camera! When light passes through the pinhole, it forms an image on the tracing paper. Find out how on the opposite page. If you used photographic paper (special paper that reacts to light) on the back of the box instead of tracing paper, a photograph would be produced. But, to see the image, you would need a darkroom and developing equipment.

Coloured sticky tape

Tracing paper

Kitchen foil

Small cardboard box with a hinged lid

You will need

Strong glue

Poster paints

EQUIPMENT

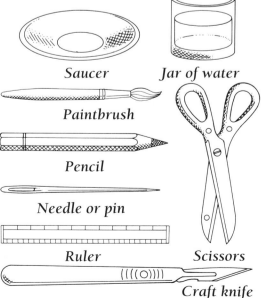

Saucer

Jar of water

Paintbrush

Pencil

Needle or pin

Scissors

Ruler

Craft knife

Making the camera

1 Gently take the box apart and paint it. Paint the inside black. Let the box dry. Ask an adult to cut a large rectangle out of one side.

2 Ask an adult to cut a small square out of the side of the box opposite the rectangle. Glue the box back together. Let it dry.

3 Tape tracing paper over the large rectangular hole and foil over the square. Prick the centre of the foil with a pin to make a hole.

The finished pinhole camera

It is difficult to make a neat pinhole through card. This is why a piece of kitchen foil is used.

Pinhole

Tape along the box edges. This gives a neat finish and stops light getting into the box.

The box must shut out the light.

Using the camera

Hold the box with the foil at the front.

You will see a stronger image if you cover your head and the back of the box with a cloth.

Point the camera towards a window or an object in bright light. You will see an upside-down image on the tracing paper.

HOW IS THE IMAGE FORMED?

Light travels in straight lines. Every object reflects some light. Here, light is reflected off the girl. It passes through the pinhole on to the tracing paper and forms a picture of the girl. If the pinhole is too big, the light will spread over a large area and form a blurred image.

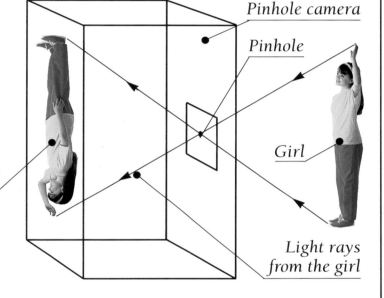

Pinhole camera

Pinhole

Girl

Girl's image on tracing paper

Light rays from the girl

The brighter the image, the easier it will be to see. Ask a friend to stand near a window so that he or she is brightly lit.

The further away the object is from the pinhole, the smaller the image will be on the tracing paper.

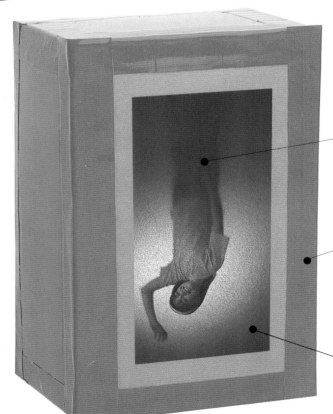

The image of the girl is upside-down and reversed.

Pinhole camera

Tracing paper

WHY IS THE IMAGE UPSIDE-DOWN?

The light coming from the girl's head passes through the pinhole in a downward direction to the bottom of the tracing paper. The light coming from the girl's feet passes through the pinhole in an upward direction to the top of the tracing paper. This happens to light from all over the girl, making the image upside-down and reversed.

CAMERA OBSCURA

Instead of a pinhole, this camera uses a magnifying glass to form a picture on tracing paper. The glass works in a similar way to the lens on a "real" camera. It lets in more light than a pinhole, so it gives a brighter image*.

You will need

Card

Tracing paper

Small cardboard box with a hinged lid

Strong glue

Coloured sticky tape

Small magnifying glass, with magnification of about x 2 (You can buy these from stationery shops.)

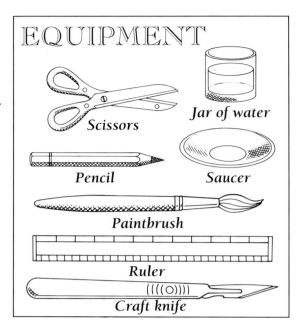

Poster paints

EQUIPMENT

Scissors

Jar of water

Pencil

Saucer

Paintbrush

Ruler

Craft knife

Making the camera

1 Gently take the box apart and paint it. Paint the inside black. Let the box dry. Ask an adult to cut a large rectangle out of one side.

2 Cut out a rectangle of card measuring 10 cm x 20 cm. Roll and tape the card to make a tube that fits the lens, as shown.

3 Hold the tube on the side of the box that is opposite the large rectangular hole. Draw round it with a pencil.

*Unlike the pinhole camera, this camera gives a sharp image with a large hole because the lens focuses the light.

The finished camera obscura

The camera obscura was developed from the pinhole camera. Camera obscuras, similar to the one you have made, were used by artists more than 400 years ago to cast an image on to a wall or canvas, which they would then copy.

Don't worry if there are small gaps around the tube. The camera will still work.

Tape along the box edges to stop light getting in.

4 Ask an adult to cut out the circle you have drawn with a craft knife. Glue the box back together and leave it to dry.

Using the camera

Point the magnifying glass towards an object that is in bright light. Push the tube in or out of the box until you see the image focused (sharp) on the tracing paper.

Focus by pushing the tube in or out.

5 Cut a piece of tracing paper to fit over the rectangular hole on one side of the box. Tape the tracing paper over the hole.

HOW DOES IT WORK?

Light rays coming from the object pass through the magnifying glass. The glass bends the rays and makes them meet (or focus) on the tracing paper, where they form a picture.

Just like the picture formed by the pinhole camera, the image on the tracing paper is upside-down and reversed.

CAMERA LENSES

Camera lenses are more complicated shapes than a magnifying glass and make even sharper pictures. Instead of tracing paper, there is light-sensitive film in a "real" camera**. When you take a photograph, an image is formed on the light-sensitive film. The photograph is then developed and printed.

Camera obscura

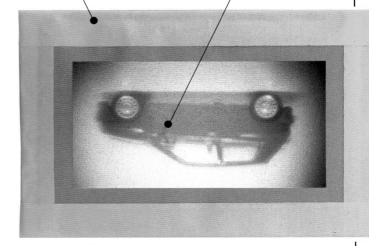

6 Slot the tube into its hole, as shown. You should be able to slide it in and out of the box. Tape the magnifying glass to the tube.

**Turn to page 11 to find out about film. 9

CAMERAS AND FILM

All cameras form an image in a similar way to the camera obscura. You will need a camera for the projects in this book.

Every camera has a lens that focuses light. When you press the shutter release button, a door opens to let light through a hole called the aperture and on to the film*. You can find out about film on the opposite page.

35 mm FIXED FOCUS CAMERA

These cameras are very popular. The lens is fixed, which means that you can only take sharp photographs from beyond a certain distance. This is explained in the camera's instructions.

These cameras usually come with a built-in flash.

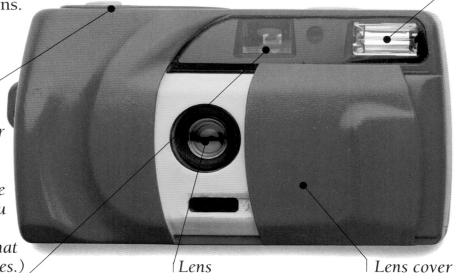

Shutter release button

Viewfinder (This is above the lens, so the picture you see is not exactly what the lens sees.)

Lens

Lens cover

110 VIEWFINDER CAMERA

110 refers to the film used in this camera, which is smaller than 35 mm film. 110 cameras are always long and thin in shape.

This camera has a switch that changes the lens setting from normal to telephoto (a lens that makes the subject appear closer).

Viewfinder

Lens

Built-in flash

35 mm SINGLE LENS REFLEX CAMERA

These expensive cameras, known as S.L.R.s, have many settings for different light conditions. Unlike other cameras, when you look into the viewfinder, you can see directly down the lens due to a special mirror inside.

Different lenses can be attached to these cameras.

You can change the focus to suit the picture. Focusing distances are marked on the lens.

Shutter release button

Rewind button

This camera has a detachable flash that clips on here.

Viewfinder

Built-in flash

The lens on this camera has a fixed focusing distance.

DISPOSABLE CAMERA

These cameras have a 35 mm film sealed inside and can only be used once. You give the camera to a film processor (a shop that develops film) where the pictures are developed and the camera is thrown away. Some disposables can take panoramas. Others can be used underwater.

The aperture hole is made bigger or smaller to let more or less light through.

FILM

Film has a light-sensitive coating. When you take a picture, light hits the film and forms an image. The amount of light reaching the film is called the exposure. Different film types are explained below.

Developing

You take finished film to a film processor. Usually, negative images are developed on the film. Then positive photographs are printed from the negatives.

Colour print

35 mm colour negative film

This film is suitable for all 35 mm cameras.

35 mm film comes in cases called cassettes.

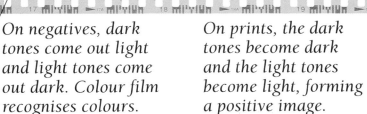

On negatives, dark tones come out light and light tones come out dark. Colour film recognises colours.

On prints, the dark tones become dark and the light tones become light, forming a positive image.

35 mm slide film

When this film is developed, the pictures you get are on film. You view them on a projector. There are no negatives.

Slide film cassette

A slide is a positive image. It comes in a plastic holder.

The standard size for 35 mm film prints is 15 cm x 10 cm (6 in. x 4 in.).

Black and white print

35 mm black and white film

Pictures from this film are in tones of black and white. It is suitable for all 35 mm cameras.

Black and white film cassette

Developed 35 mm black and white negatives

Smaller prints (12.5 cm x 10 cm; 5 in. x 4 in.) are produced from 110 film.

110 colour film

110 cameras take this film.

110 film comes in a cartridge. You don't have to pull any film out of the cartridge when you load a 110 film.

Smaller negatives are produced from 110 film.

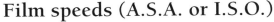

Film speeds (A.S.A. or I.S.O.)

Film comes in different speeds for different light conditions. A film's speed is shown by its A.S.A. or I.S.O. number. A film with a high number is better for low light conditions**.

How many frames?

You can buy films with 12, 24, or 36 frames (the number of pictures you can take with a film).

**Generally, it is best to buy 200 A.S.A./I.S.O.

TAKING PICTURES

Once you have a camera and film, you're ready to take photographs. Read the instructions that come with your camera so that you know how to use it, and check if your camera needs batteries.

Here you can find some tips and ideas to help you take good photographs. Don't worry if some of your photographs go wrong. The important thing is to have fun and experiment.

If you have a camera strap, keep it round your neck or wrist.

Your hair, fingers, and camera strap must be away from the lens and flash.

Ready to shoot

Look carefully through your viewfinder and decide what you want in your picture. Keep the camera still or the shot might be blurred.

Keep your elbows close to your body.

Stand with your legs slightly apart.

Portrait or landscape

You can create different picture shapes or formats by holding your camera in different ways. Portrait and landscape are the most commonly used formats, but you can use any angle you wish. Turn the camera to see which way your subject best fills your viewfinder.

Look through your viewfinder to work out the best way to hold your camera to take the picture.

TAKING PORTRAITS

When you hold a camera like this, the photograph you take will be a "portrait". This means that the longer sides of the photograph will be upright.

Landscape

When the picture is taken this way, there is empty space on either side of the girl. So a "portrait" is the best choice here.

Portrait

In this "portrait" picture, the girl fills the photograph.

Landscape

TAKING LANDSCAPES

When you hold a camera like this, the photograph you take will be a "landscape". This means that the shorter sides of the photograph will be upright.

Odd angle portrait

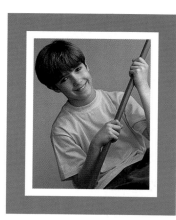

USING ODD ANGLES

When you hold a camera like this, the subject will be at an angle. The picture can be "portrait" or "landscape".

Viewpoint

The position from which you take a picture is called the viewpoint. Try out different viewpoints. Kneel down or stand on a chair, get closer or further away.

Try crouching down low or lying down and looking up at a friend.

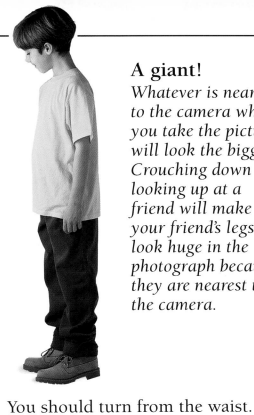

A giant!

Whatever is nearest to the camera when you take the picture will look the biggest. Crouching down and looking up at a friend will make your friend's legs look huge in the photograph because they are nearest to the camera.

Panning

Try taking a photograph of a moving subject using a technique called panning. Look through your viewfinder and follow the subject.

You should turn from the waist. Press your shutter release button while your camera is moving at the same speed as the subject.

Keep the moving subject in your viewfinder, and take the picture as you move. The background will be blurred, giving an idea of speed, but the moving subject will be in focus.

Loading batteries and film

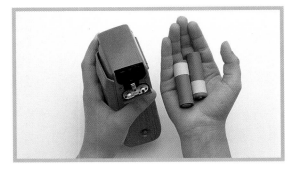

Check your camera's instructions to find out if it needs batteries. Use the correct type and number of batteries*.

*Always take out the batteries if you are not going to use your camera for a long time.

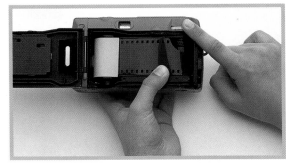

Follow your camera's instructions for loading film. Once the film is in the camera, don't open the camera until you have rewound the film**.

**When loading 35 mm film, you need to pull a little of the film out of the cassette.

When you reach the last frame, rewind the film. This is either done automatically or by hand. Check your camera's instructions.

FAVOURITE PHOTOS

When you look at your photographs, you will have lots of favourites for different reasons. Some will remind you of holidays, friends, or family. Others will show interesting effects. Even photographs that go wrong can make funny or creative pictures. Here are some examples.

BEST FRIENDS

It's great to have photographs of your friends and family that you can keep and display around you.

BLURRED

This photograph is out of focus because the photographer moved when taking the picture. But it shows the party fun.

RAINDROPS

Raindrops fell on the lens when this photograph was taken, making a perfect rainy day picture. But remember: you must always try to keep your camera dry.

Take your time and find a good view when taking pictures of places.

IN AND OUT OF FOCUS

Here the photographer has focused on the flowers in the distance and deliberately made the railing out of focus, creating an interesting effect.

14

The blurred effect adds to the party feel!

Look for an interesting viewpoint.

VIEWPOINTS
A photograph can look interesting taken from an unusual viewpoint. Here, the photographer has taken a picture of a young boy through a colourful climbing frame.

PLACES
You can show photographs of places you have visited to your friends.

FUNNY PHOTOS
You should check the background before taking a picture. But, sometimes, if you don't, you get a funny picture like this.

ANIMALS
Animals can be difficult subjects. Just when you are about to take their picture, they run off! This picture was taken from overhead. The stretched-out cat looks unbelievably long.

15

CROPPING AND ENLARGING

Sometimes you can improve a photograph by making part of it bigger and cropping (removing) the rest. "Croppers" (two pieces of L-shaped card) will help you to decide what to crop and what shape the new picture should be. The print you use must be sharp or the enlargement will be blurred.

EQUIPMENT

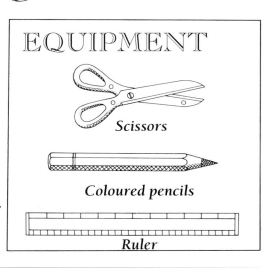

Scissors

Coloured pencils

Ruler

You will need

Template for both halves of the croppers

Trace this black outline.

Masking tape

Thick black card

Tracing paper

Sticky tape for strengthening the croppers

White paper

Thick coloured card

Negative of the print

Print to be cropped

Cropping the print

1 Trace the template and colour over your lines. Turn over the tracing paper and place it on black card. Draw over your lines twice.

2 Cut out the croppers. Fold a piece of tracing paper round your print and tape it to the back of the print with masking tape.

3 Use the croppers to mark the part of the print you want to enlarge*. Take the negative and marked print to a film processor.

*Draw round your chosen area on the tracing paper. Write on the size of print you want.

The finished print

Remember that cropping and enlarging is not done just to make one part of a photograph bigger. It should also help the picture to tell a story. This cropped photograph focuses on the person who is about to climb the sand-dune. It makes you wonder what lies beyond the dune, and if the person will make it to the top.

The print is glued on to white paper and coloured card, creating a frame.

THE CROPPERS

You can make your cropped picture portrait, landscape, or square**. Move the croppers around the picture and slide them together or apart until they frame part of the photograph that you think will make a better picture. You can even tilt the croppers to slant the photograph!

ENLARGEMENTS

Most good film processors offer a cropping and enlarging service, but you must give them the negative and the print to work from. Check the print sizes they can make and remember that the larger the print you ask for, the more expensive it will be.

Strengthen the edges of the croppers with sticky tape.

**Turn to page 12 to find out about these different formats.

17

SPECIAL EFFECTS

Here you can find out how to make your own filters using cellophane or sweet wrappers. A filter changes the light that passes through the camera lens. Use coloured filters to create dramatic pictures and a starburst filter to fill photographs of lights with dazzling stars.

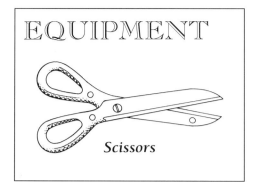

EQUIPMENT

Scissors

Making coloured filters

Tape a small square of coloured sweet wrapper over your camera lens (be careful not to touch the lens). Take the picture, as normal.

Making starburst filters

1 Dab petroleum jelly on to a square of cellophane. Wipe the petroleum jelly in one diagonal direction with tissue (press hard).

2 Turn over the cellophane. Dab on more jelly and wipe in the opposite direction, making an "X". Tape it to the lens. Take a picture*.

*Keep the cellophane flat so that the petroleum jelly doesn't touch the lens.

You will need

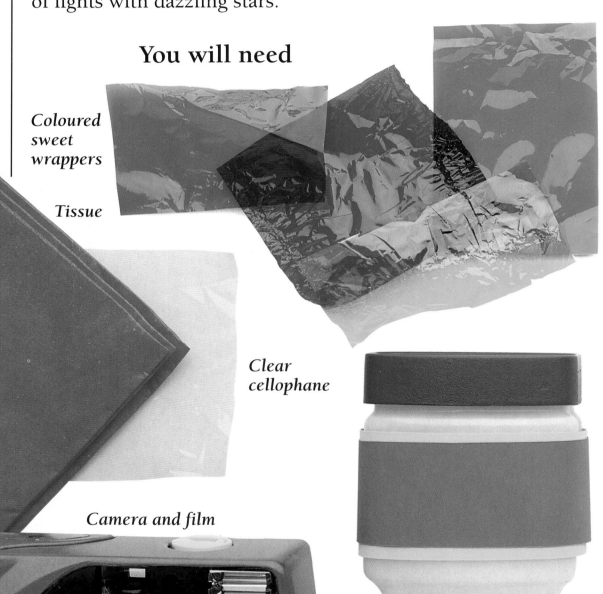

Coloured sweet wrappers

Tissue

Clear cellophane

Camera and film

Petroleum jelly

Coloured sticky tape

The finished photographs
Coloured filters
Look for a subject to photograph that has areas of bright light and areas of dark light, such as a tree with strong light behind it.

No filter used

Green sweet wrapper filter used
The filter gives the landscape an eerie glow.

Purple sweet wrapper filter used
You could try using purple or red sweet wrappers to create an amazing sunset glow in your photographs.

Two-colour filter used
Combine two different coloured sweet wrappers like this to make a two-colour picture.

Starburst filter used
Choose a subject with bright lights (a night-time scene with street lamps or car headlamps is ideal). Each light looks like an "X", like the "X" made on the cellophane.

Lens care
Never touch your lens. If you get petroleum jelly on it, clean it gently with a special lens wipe**.

**You can buy these from photographic shops.

CLOSE-UP LENS

You usually need an expensive S.L.R. camera to take close-up pictures. If you are nearer than 1 m to a subject, most fixed focus, 110, or disposable cameras will not focus. Here we show you how to use a magnifying glass to take brilliant close-up pictures with these cameras.

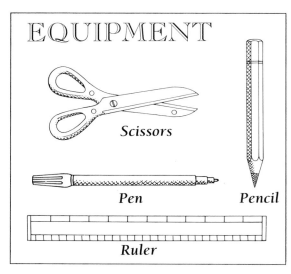

EQUIPMENT

Scissors

Pen

Pencil

Ruler

You will need

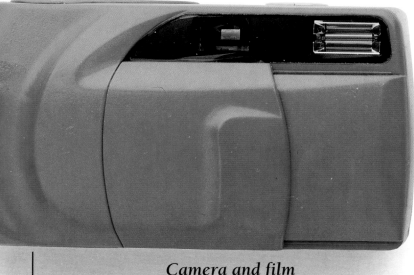

Camera and film

Modelling clay

Clear acetate (You can buy this from good stationery or art and craft shops.)

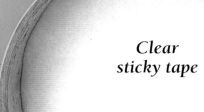

Clear sticky tape

Small magnifying glass, with magnification of about x 2 (You can buy these from stationery shops.)

Making the lens

1 Hold a magnifying glass higher or lower until you can see an object in focus. Note the distance from the glass to the object.

2 Cut a square of clear acetate and roll it to make a wide cone*. Tape the cone securely with clear sticky tape.

3 Trim down the point of the cone until the glass can be taped to it. Cut a notch for the handle of the glass, as shown.

We have used card instead of acetate so that you can see what to do. You must use clear acetate.

4 The length of the cone (from the top to the base) should be the same as the distance measured in step 1. Mark on this distance.

5 Trim the base of the cone all round to where you have marked. Make sure the base is flat and even.

6 Place a roll of modelling clay around the glass. Press firmly to stick the glass over the camera lens. Don't touch the camera lens.

Using the lens

You don't need to look through the viewfinder.

Take your close-up photographs outside in sunlight or use your camera's flash indoors. Place the cone over the subject and press the shutter release button. Choose flat or small objects that fit under the cone.

Some finished photographs

Shells

The finished lens

Light passes through the acetate cone and lights the subject. When you have finished taking close-up pictures, remove the close-up lens and modelling clay from your camera.

Modelling clay

Place the magnifying glass in front of the lens. Make sure that it is held firmly by the modelling clay.

FOCUSING TEST

Objects placed at the base of the cone should be in focus. Take a few pictures as a test, holding an object at the base of the cone and then a little nearer or further away. Adjust the length of the cone if necessary.

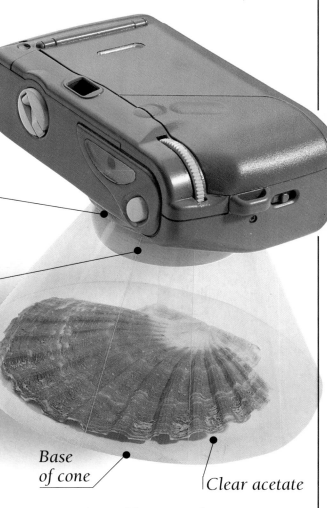

Base of cone

Clear acetate

Pins on blue paper

Marbles on red corrugated card

CAMERA CASE

Make a special case for your camera and other photographic equipment so that you can take all the things you need with you when you go out taking photographs. The case has a handle so that you can carry it comfortably, and separate compartments to make everything easy to find. You will need a sturdy shoe box with a lid to make the case. Line the box with flame retardant foam to protect your camera. You can buy this from most upholsterers.

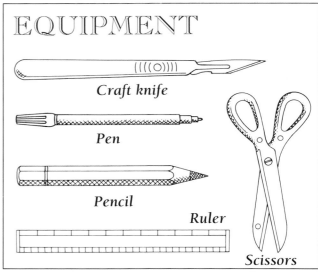

EQUIPMENT

Craft knife

Pen

Pencil

Ruler

Scissors

You will need

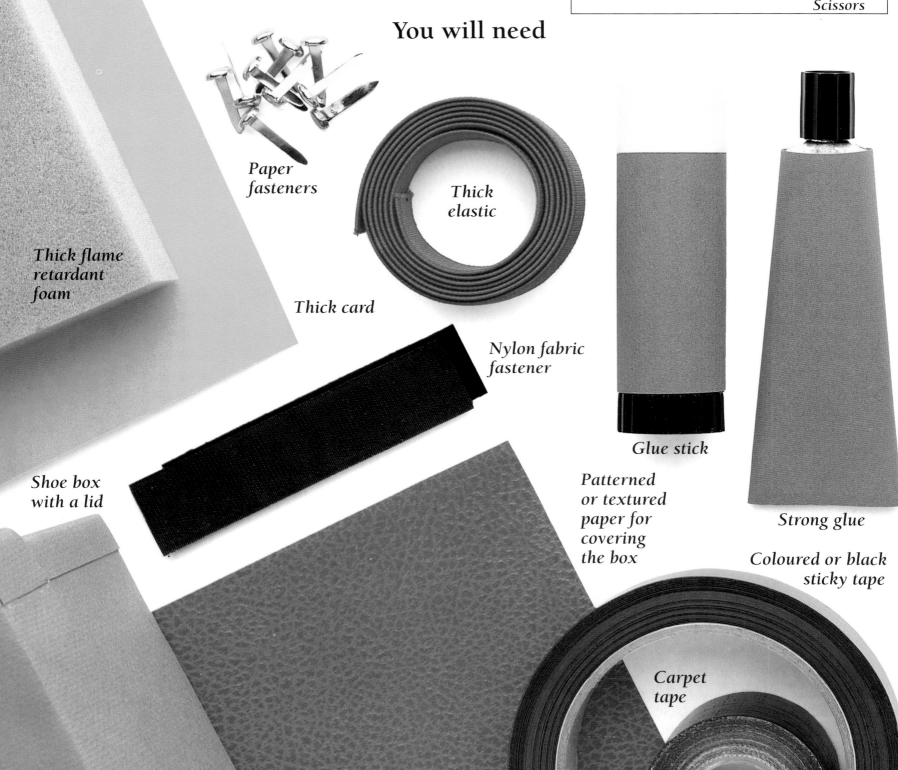

Paper fasteners

Thick elastic

Thick flame retardant foam

Thick card

Nylon fabric fastener

Glue stick

Shoe box with a lid

Patterned or textured paper for covering the box

Strong glue

Coloured or black sticky tape

Carpet tape

Making the case

1 Measure each side of the box. Cut sheets of paper exactly to these sizes. Glue them to each side of the box. Tape the box edges.

2 Make a hinge with carpet tape to hold the lid on the box. Use short vertical strips of tape on the inside of the box and lid, as shown.

3 Fix long strips of carpet tape to the outside of the box and lid to make the other side of the hinge. Use a few strips to make it strong.

4 Ask an adult to help you fix a length of elastic around the box with paper fasteners, as shown. It should fit snugly around the box.

5 Cover the paper fastener ends with carpet tape. Glue a strip of fabric fastener round the edge of the lid, in the middle, as shown.

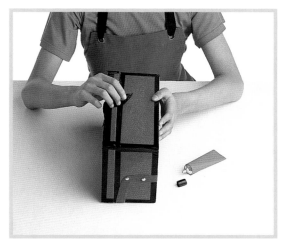

6 Glue another strip of fabric fastener in the middle of the matching side of the box. Line it up with the fabric fastener on the lid.

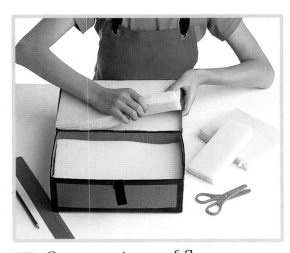

7 Cut two pieces of flame retardant foam to fit inside the box. Line the lid and the base of the box with the foam, as shown*.

8 Put your equipment in the case. Where you want partitions, mark the foam in the base with a pen and then cut along the lines.

9 Cut thick card to the width and twice the height of the case. Fold the card to make the partitions and slot them into the case**.

*If your box is deep you may need two pieces of foam in the base.
**Slot the partitions into the cuts you have made in the foam.

Photographer's Kit

The finished camera case is a safe and secure place for storing your photographic equipment. There's room for your camera, film, colour and starburst filters*, and a notebook. Cut small pieces of foam and place them on either side of your camera to stop it from sliding around.

PROTECTING YOUR CAMERA

The case stops dust and dirt getting inside your camera, while the foam protects it from knocks and bumps. But remember: never leave your camera in very hot or cold conditions. It's also a good idea to wrap your camera in a plastic bag when you take it to the beach.

Keep the lens cover closed and take out the batteries when your camera is not in use.

FILM

You can keep spare film in your case. You might also want to carry some spare batteries for your camera.

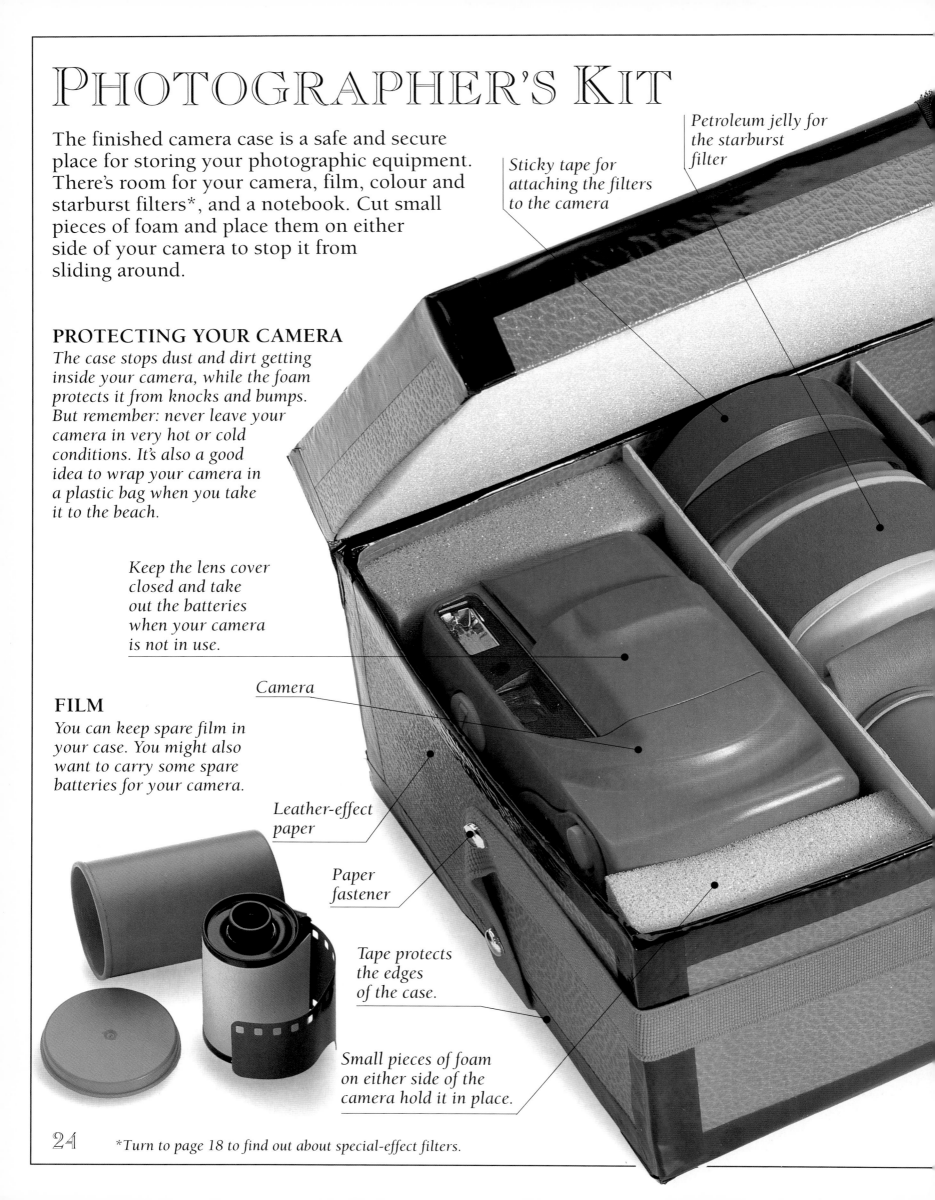

Petroleum jelly for the starburst filter

Sticky tape for attaching the filters to the camera

Camera

Leather-effect paper

Paper fastener

Tape protects the edges of the case.

Small pieces of foam on either side of the camera hold it in place.

Turn to page 18 to find out about special-effect filters.

Make sure the foam fits tightly inside the box and lid.

Carrying the case

PHOTO NOTES
Keep a record of the photographs you take in a notebook. You can write down the frame number, what was in the shot, the date, and the type of filter used (if you used one).

Notebook and pencil

Hold the strap like this when you want to carry the case**.

PAPER COVERING
We have used a leather-effect paper to cover the shoe box. You can buy different patterned or textured papers from art and craft or stationery shops. Make sure the box you use is made of thick card.

DIVIDING THE CASE
Before you make the partitions, put all your equipment in the camera case and work out the best way to divide up the case.

Card partitions

Tissue for the starburst filter

Spare film

Filters

Wrap the handle round the sides of the case when you want to open the lid.

This length of fabric fastener sticks to the piece on the lid and holds the case shut.

FILTER FILE
Make a small file for your filters out of card. Fasten it with a paper fastener, as shown.

**The case is not suitable for heavy cameras.

MIX AND MATCH

You don't have to use just one photograph to make a picture. Why not take several photographs and join them together to make a panorama or montage?

A panorama is a series of photographs of the same view, which are matched up to make one long picture. A montage is a mixture of different photographs that are stuck together. Here squares are cut out of old photographs, showing things such as people, colours, and textures.

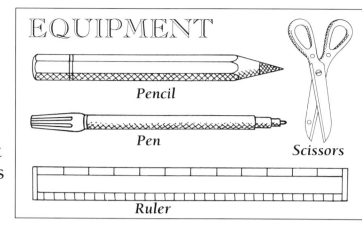

Pencil

Pen

Scissors

Ruler

You will need

Old prints for montage

Croppers

Masking tape

White paper

Glue stick

Thick coloured card

Prints for panorama

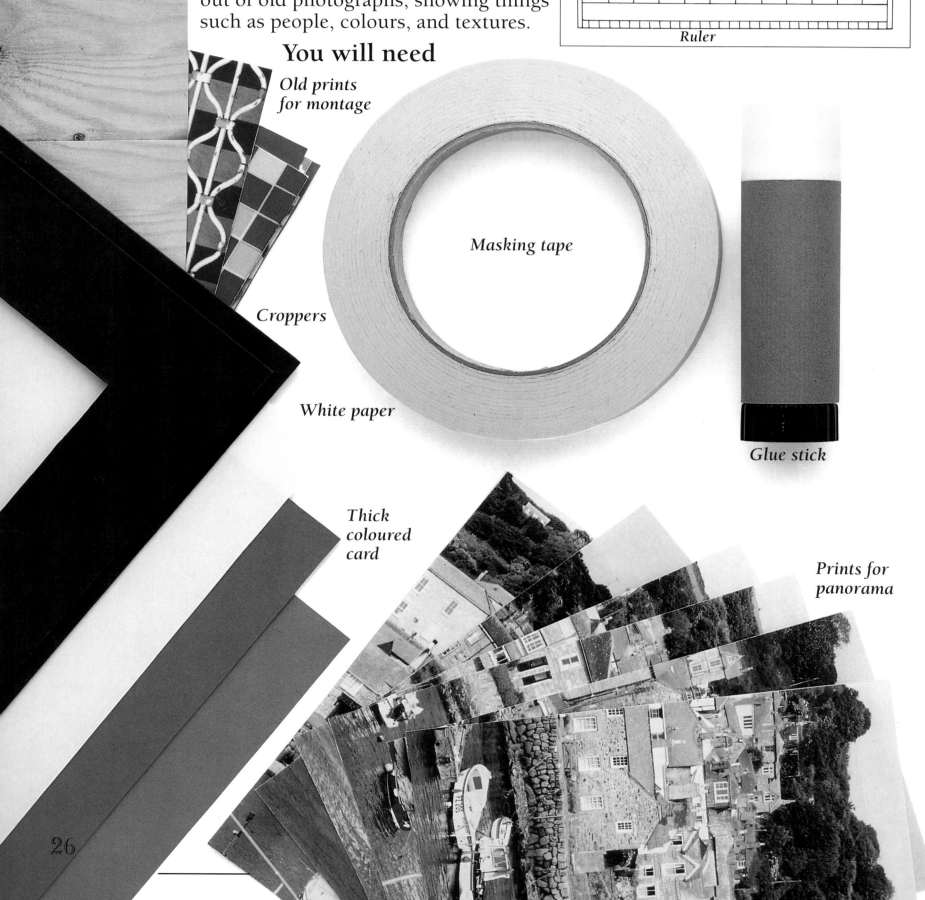

Taking a panorama

1 Choose a view to photograph and decide where you want your panorama to start and finish. Stand where you can see the whole view and do not move from this spot while taking the panorama. Turn your body from the waist so that you can see the start of the view in your viewfinder. Take the first picture.

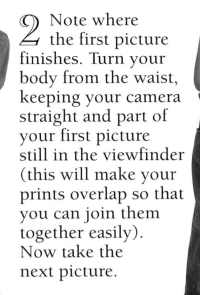

2 Note where the first picture finishes. Turn your body from the waist, keeping your camera straight and part of your first picture still in the viewfinder (this will make your prints overlap so that you can join them together easily). Now take the next picture.

3 Carry on like this, turning your body a little bit more and taking another picture after each turn, until you have photographed the whole view. Remember to hold your camera firmly and to wind on your film after every shot, if your camera doesn't do this automatically.

Making a panorama

1 Lay down the first two prints and match them up. Tape them together with masking tape. Do this with all of the prints.

2 When you have taped together all of the prints, turn over the panorama and tape the prints on the back. Remove the tape on the front.

3 Rule lines along the top and bottom of the panorama to give a neat finish. Carefully cut along these lines with scissors.

Making a montage

4 Glue the prints on to white or coloured paper to create a narrow border. Then glue the panorama on to card, as shown.

1 Use your croppers to find interesting parts of old prints. Draw 3 cm squares around the parts of the prints and cut them out.

2 Arrange the squares and glue them on to a sheet of white paper. Then glue the sheet of paper on to some coloured card.

THE FINISHED PICTURES

The finished panorama and montage will make impressive pictures for your bedroom wall. You could make a montage of the people in your family to give to your parents as a present. Look through your old photographs for the montage pictures. You could also look for images in magazines.

MONTAGE MIXTURES

You can use photographs of friends, animals, textures, or colours, or a mixture of all of these, in a montage. Together, the small square images create a colourful picture.

A border of white paper helps the montage to stand out.

PANORAMIC PICTURE

Match up your prints carefully. The finished panorama will look like one long picture.

Take as many photographs as you need to complete the view.

Here, photographs of such things as paper clips, plants, pebbles, and lentils, make a montage of contrasting textures.

Coloured card creates a frame.

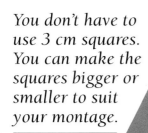

You don't have to use 3 cm squares. You can make the squares bigger or smaller to suit your montage.

Different faces, some smiling, some eating, some laughing, make a fun montage.

USING OLD PRINTS

A montage is a clever way of using old photographs that are not good enough to frame or put in an album, but are too interesting to throw away.

MATCHING UP

Don't worry if your panorama doesn't match up exactly. It will still look like one picture.

Portrait or landscape photographs can be used in a panorama*. Here, portrait photographs were used.

*Turn to page 12 to find out about these different formats.

29

PHOTO COLLAGE

Making a colourful collage using photographs of flowers and other natural objects is easy and lots of fun! Look in your garden, a window box, or a local park for plants to photograph*. For the background, photograph bright colours or interesting textures, such as the sky or a wall. Make sure you take several frames of the background photographs.

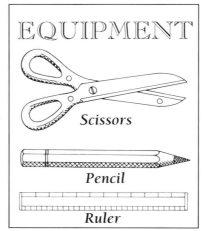

EQUIPMENT

Scissors

Pencil

Ruler

Prints for the background (We have used a rough plaster wall and the sky.)

You will need

Glue stick

White card

Prints of flowers, leaves, fruit, vegetables, shells, or other natural objects

Thick coloured card

Making the collage

1 Cut out some white card to the size that you want to make your collage. Glue the background prints to the card.

2 Cut out the flowers and other objects that you want to use from your prints. Glue them down. Don't be afraid to overlap images.

3 Once you are happy with your picture, glue the collage on to thick coloured card, creating a border about 2.5 cm wide.

Check your camera's minimum focusing distance and stand as near to the objects as you can when you take the pictures.

The finished collage

Try using photographs of a variety of natural objects. We have used fruit, berries, vegetables, and a shell, as well as flowers. You could even add photographs of trees!

Photograph of a bottle

Photograph of the sky

Photographs of flowers, berries, and leaves

Leave a narrow border of white card.

The border of red card frames the collage.

THE BACKGROUND

For a different background, try using photographs of a lawn, tree bark, or a table.

Photographs of fruit, a shell, and other natural objects

Photograph of a rough plaster wall

Different shapes, sizes, textures, and colours create an exciting picture.

31

CONCERTINA CARD

When you write to friends or relatives, why not send some photographs, too, showing the things you have done. Here, you can find out how to make a special photographic card to write a letter on.

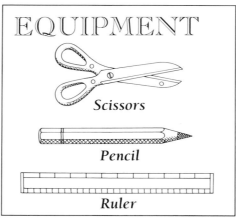
You will need

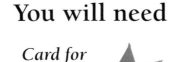

Card for flap

Writing paper

Ribbon

Card for the concertina section

Hole punch

Glue stick

3 prints (standard size: 15 cm x 10 cm; 6 in. x 4 in.)

Making the card

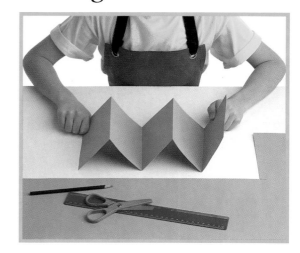

1 Cut out a 52.5 cm x 15 cm rectangle of card. Fold the card into five sections, each measuring 10.5 cm*. Fold the card, as shown.

2 Glue 10.5 cm x 15 cm sheets of writing paper to four sections of the card. Glue an 8 cm x 15 cm strip of card to one end.

3 Fold over the strip of card to make a flap and angle the corners. Glue three prints to the other side of the card, as shown.

This will make a concertina card for three 15 cm x 10 cm (6 in. x 4 in.) prints.

The finished concertina card

When you have written your letter on the writing paper, punch a hole in the flap at the end of the concertina card. Thread a ribbon through the hole and round the folded card. Finally, tie the ribbon in a bow to hold the card together.

POST IT

If you are posting your card, put it into an envelope, write on the address, and add a stamp.

When tied, the ribbon holds the folded card together.

Photographs

Hole made by a hole punch

Write the name of the person you are sending the card to on the front.

AN EXTRA SET

If you want to keep a set of the photographs you are using, take the negatives to a film processor (a shop that develops film) and get reprints made.

Flap with angled corners

A PHOTOGRAPHIC DISPLAY

Your friend can hang the card on a wall or stand it up on a shelf or mantelpiece.

Ribbon

CONCERTINA FOLDS

The concertina card is folded like a concertina (a type of musical instrument).

You can make a longer card with more photographs by adding more sections. You can also adjust the size of the card for larger or smaller prints.

PLAY THEATRE

Why not use photographs and pictures from old magazines to make characters and scenery for a play theatre? Include photographs of yourself, so that you can be in the play, too.

Below, standard sized prints, enlarged prints, and pictures from old magazines are used to create a fantasy world of little people, with giant garden scenery and a giant cat. If you don't have any photographs for scenery look for pictures in old magazines or catalogues. Turn the page for some ideas for other scenes.

EQUIPMENT

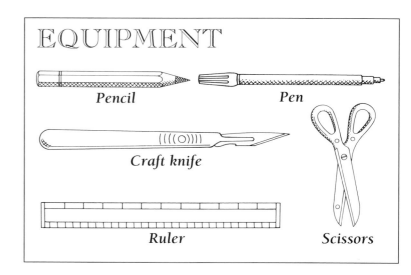

Pencil

Pen

Craft knife

Ruler

Scissors

You will need

Coloured paper

Glue stick

Standard sized prints (15 cm x 10 cm; 6 in. x 4 in.)

Coloured card

Corrugated card box or shoe box

Enlarged prints

Old magazines or catalogues

34

Making the theatre

1 Cover the box by gluing coloured paper to the inside and outside. When dry, cut sections from the box sides, as shown.

2 Glue prints to the base of the box theatre for the ground. Glue paper grass shapes to the back and around the box edges.

3 Cut out the objects that you are going to use as scenery. If you don't have enlarged prints, find images in magazines or catalogues.

4 Glue the cut-out objects on to card. When the glue is dry, draw a flap at the base of each piece of scenery, as shown.

5 Cut round the pieces of scenery and their flaps. Score and fold the flaps to make the objects stand up and place them in the theatre.

6 Glue photographs of people and of a giant animal on to card*. Cut them out. Cut a slit in the feet of each cut-out person.

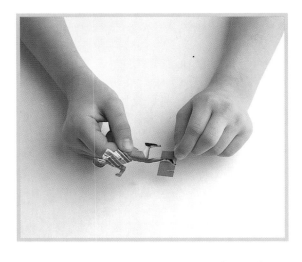

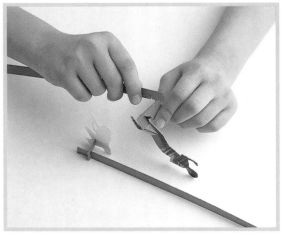

7 Cut small rectangles of card and make two slits in either side, as shown. Slot the characters' feet into one of the slits.

*If you don't have an enlarged print, use a picture from an old magazine or catalogue.

8 Cut long strips of card for your characters. Cut a slit into one end of each strip. Slot the characters on to the strips of card, as shown.

9 Ask an adult to cut a slit along the top and down one side of the box that is big enough for the giant animal to fit into.

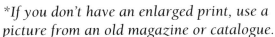

ACT OUT A STORY

You can make as many characters as you need and add more pieces of scenery. Set up your finished theatre on a table and you are ready to act out an adventure story. Make up what happens as you go along or write a script and present the play to your friends. Will your characters escape from the land of the giants?

OTHER IDEAS FOR SCENES

You don't have to make a "land of the giants" play theatre. You can make any scene you like. Try using photographs taken at the zoo, farm, or in your home to make an animal or room scene.

EXTRA PHOTOGRAPHS

If you don't have all the images you need, look for photographs in old magazines or catalogues.

Coloured paper covers the back of the box.

Layers of paper grass shapes create a background and decorate the edge of the box.

Photographs of grass are used on the base of the theatre.

GIANT ANIMAL

You can give the negative of your own animal photograph to a film processor to enlarge, or have it enlarged on a colour photocopier at a photocopying shop*. Alternatively, look for a large photograph of an animal in magazines or catalogues, or paint a giant animal on card.

The giant animal peeps in at the characters from above.

Scenery

Characters

Using the play theatre

Move your characters around the scene using the long strips of card, so that your hands don't get in the way. Slide the giant animal in and out of the box.

THE SCENERY

You can glue the flaps that support the scenery to the base of the theatre, if you don't want to change your set for different adventures.

THE CHARACTERS

Ask your friends to act out parts of your story when you take their photographs. They can look frightened, happy, pretend to run, or sit on the floor. Get a friend to take your picture so that you can be in the story, too.

Long strips of card

*Remember that the bigger the enlargement, the more expensive it will be.

Photo Frames

Display your favourite photographs in fabulous stand-up photo frames! Below are instructions for making a frame for a 15 cm x 10 cm (6 in. x 4 in.) standard size print. You can increase or reduce the size of this frame for larger or smaller prints. You can also make the format portrait or landscape by adapting the frame measurements to suit the format of your photograph. (Turn to page 12 to find out about different formats.)

(Turn to page 12 to find out about different formats.)

EQUIPMENT

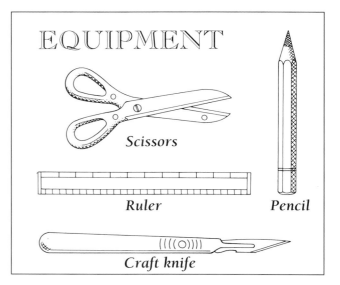

Scissors

Ruler

Pencil

Craft knife

You will need

Coloured card

Squares of coloured paper for decoration

Patterned or textured paper for decoration

Strong glue

Small beads for decoration

Making the frames

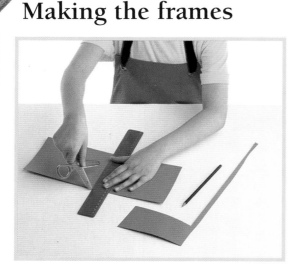

1 Cut out a rectangle of card 13 cm x 34 cm*. Measure halfway across the card and score along the middle mark.

2 Fold the card in half. Draw a rectangle in one half of the card with a 2 cm border all around it. Ask an adult to cut it out.

3 Glue a rectangle of card 16.5 cm x 12 cm inside the frame, over the hole. Glue along the short edges only, as shown.

This will make a portrait frame big enough to frame a 15 cm x 10 cm (6 in. x 4 in.) print.

4 Cut out a thin strip of card about 18 cm long. Make a fold at one end. Glue the strip to the inside of the frame, as shown.

5 Ask an adult to make a slit in the other side of the frame. Slot the strip of card through the slit to make the frame stand up.

6 For decoration, glue on beads, textured paper, or paper cut-outs. When dry, slide a print into the side of the frame, as shown.

The finished frames

Here are some finished frames with photographs. They make great gifts for friends or family. Choose one of your best photographs to frame. You may need to trim the edges of the photograph so that it fits in the frame.

Colourful beads have been glued to this frame. You could also use dried beans, pasta, or shells.

A border of yellow card helps this photograph to stand out.

Try gluing patterned or textured paper to a frame. Cut the paper to fit the frame and angle the corners, as shown.

The cut-out paper shapes glued on to this frame make a pretty decoration.

PHOTO ALBUM

Make the most of your best photographs by displaying them in a photo album. You can make an album using a ring-binder, card, and tissue paper. The tissue paper will protect the prints, which are held in place with photo corners. The album also has pockets for your negatives. The pockets will keep your negatives clean and safe, so that you can use them for reprints or enlargements.

Coloured sticky tape

Sticky labels

You will need

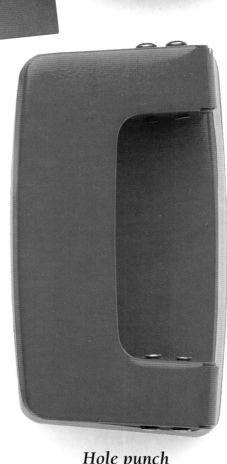

Hole punch

EQUIPMENT

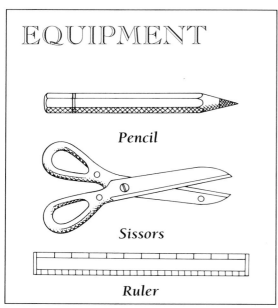

Pencil

Sissors

Ruler

Photo corners (You can buy these from stationery shops.)

Making the album

1 Cut out sheets of black card to make pages that fit your ring-binder. Cut sheets of tissue paper, double the page size, as shown.

2 Fold the sheets of tissue paper round the sheets of card. Punch holes through the finished pages and put them into the binder.

3 Cut out sheets of coloured card to the same size as the sheets of black card. Punch holes through these as well.

40

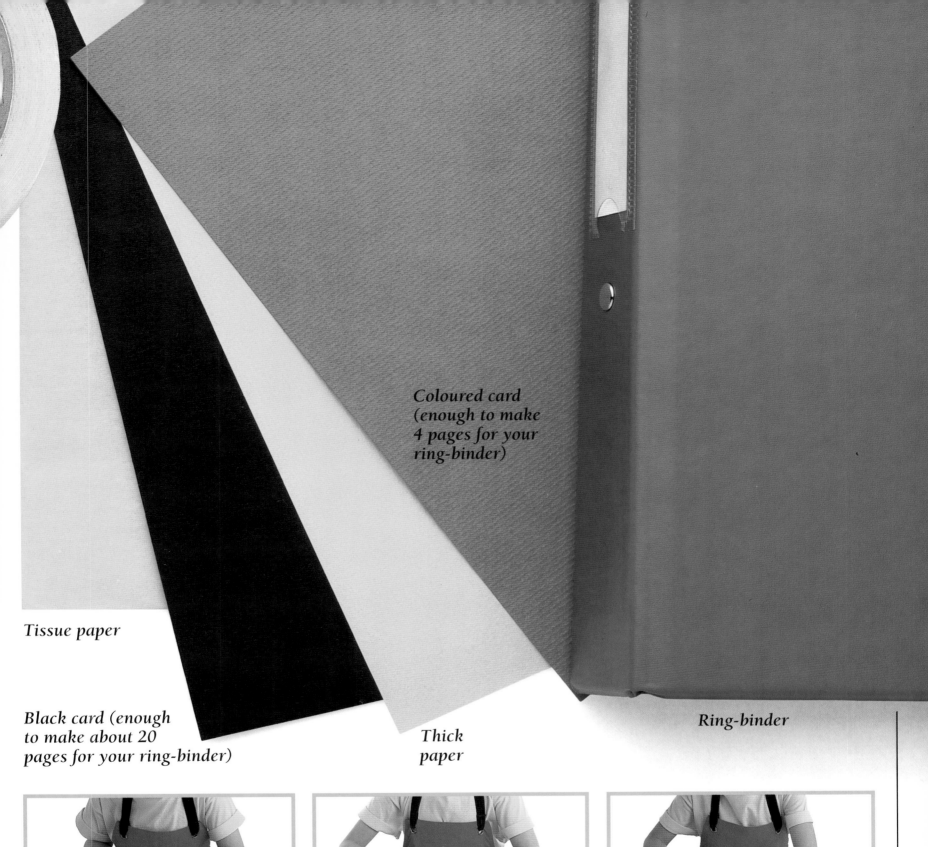

Tissue paper

Coloured card
(enough to make
4 pages for your
ring-binder)

Black card (enough
to make about 20
pages for your ring-binder)

Thick
paper

Ring-binder

4 Tape rectangles of paper on three sides to the coloured card to make pockets*. Put the sheets of card into the ring-binder.

5 Arrange your photographs on the black pages. Use photo corners to stick them down. Stick labels under each photograph.

6 Put the negatives of your photographs into the paper pockets. Stick labels under each negative pocket.

*The rectangles should measure about 10 cm x 20 cm.

41

STORING YOUR PHOTOS

The ring-binder album will hold many photographs and negatives. You can add more sheets of card and tissue paper as you need them. Try to keep the album up to date. It will become a record of what you've seen and done to show to your family and friends.

Photo corner

LABELS

Label your prints. You can say where and when the picture was taken, who or what is in the photograph, and if a filter was used.

You can also match each print with the set of negatives it comes from. Label your sets of negatives (A,B,C, etc.). Then label each print with its frame number and the set of negatives it comes from.

With Josey on my birthday 15 may 1994 A12

Car wheel, August 1994 B20

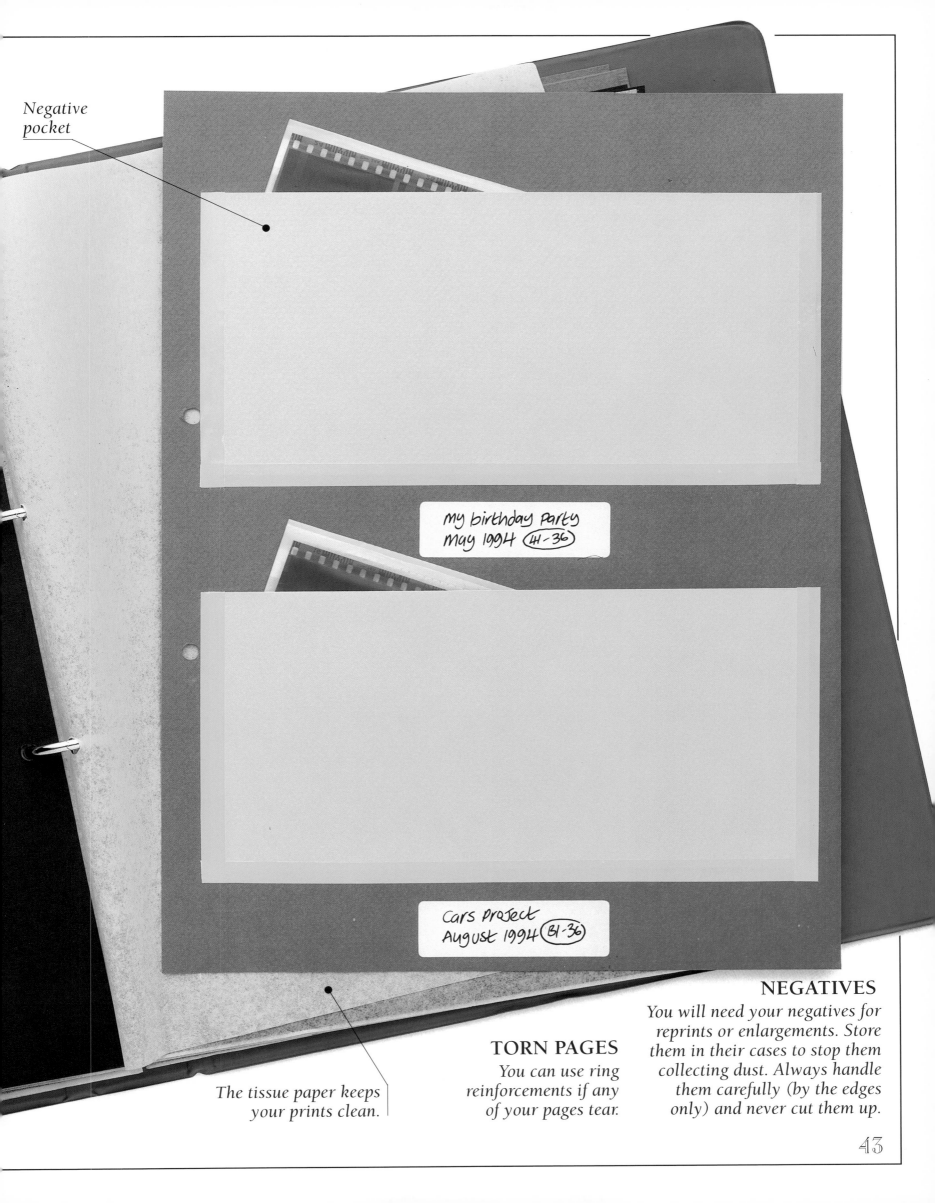

Negative pocket

my birthday party
May 1994 (4-36)

Cars project
August 1994 (31-36)

TORN PAGES
You can use ring
reinforcements if any
of your pages tear.

The tissue paper keeps
your prints clean.

NEGATIVES
You will need your negatives for
reprints or enlargements. Store
them in their cases to stop them
collecting dust. Always handle
them carefully (by the edges
only) and never cut them up.

43

MAKE IT MOVE!

When you look at a sequence of action photographs passing quickly before your eyes, the images look as if they are moving, just like a film at the cinema. You can see this effect by looking into a machine called a zoetrope. Before you make the zoetrope, you will need to take 13 photographs showing someone doing each stage of a simple action. Below, photographs of a clown lifting his hat and then putting it back on are used.

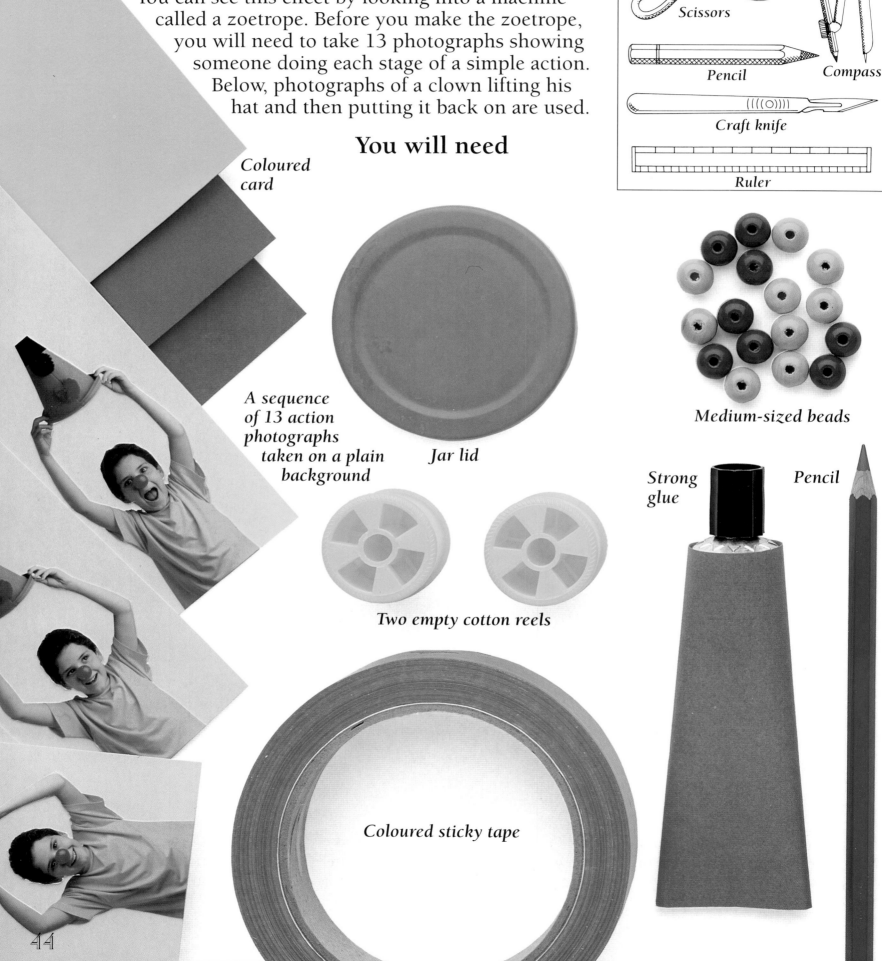

EQUIPMENT

Scissors

Compass

Pencil

Craft knife

Ruler

You will need

Coloured card

A sequence of 13 action photographs taken on a plain background

Jar lid

Medium-sized beads

Two empty cotton reels

Strong glue

Pencil

Coloured sticky tape

Making the zoetrope

1 Use a compass to draw a circle with a radius of 12.5 cm on card. Cut it out. Draw round a cotton reel in the circle's centre.

2 Ask an adult to cut slightly within the cotton reel circle, making a hole that the cotton reel fits into without sliding out.

3 Glue one cotton reel on to the inside of a jar lid and one to the outside. Glue a pencil into the reel on the outside of the lid.

4 Cut a strip of card 11.5 cm x 81 cm*. Measure 0.5 cm wide slots every 5.5 cm. Mark them all along one edge of the card.

5 Mark each of the 0.5 cm wide slots to be 4 cm deep. Use a ruler to draw the slots neatly. Cut them out.

6 Overlap the ends of the slotted card by 2 cm and glue them to make a tube. Tape the circle of card to the tube to make a base.

7 Trim the prints to make small rectangles and stick them on to a strip of card 7.5 cm x 80 cm**. Leave a 2 cm gap at one end.

8 Overlap the card by 2 cm and glue it to make a tube with the prints on the inside. Put the card in the drum, and beads in the jar lid.

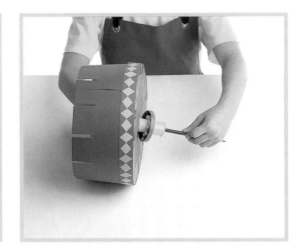

9 Push the cotton reel through the hole in the base of the drum. It should fit snugly. The zoetrope is now ready to spin!

*You can stick two strips of card together to make it stronger. We have used yellow and blue card.

**The cut-out prints should measure 6 cm x 6 cm. Stick them down in order to make an action sequence.

45

THE FINISHED ZOETROPE

When you spin the drum and look through the slits, the pictures will appear to move! The drum spins on the loose beads in the jar lid. Try making several action sequences to place inside your zoetrope. You and your friends will have lots of fun seeing each other in action.

THE ZOETROPE PHOTOGRAPHS

Ask a friend to wear bright colours that will show up well and to stand against a plain background. The plain background will help you to join the photographs together easily. Take the photographs outside on a sunny day or use your camera's flash indoors.

When you glue your action photographs on to card, leave a thin border of card at the top and bottom. This will help your photographs to stand out.

Blue and yellow sheets of card were stuck together to make this zoetrope. Using two sheets makes the drum stronger.

A SIMPLE ACTION

Keep your action shots simple. Someone waving, clapping, or taking off a hat, as shown here, are easy shots to take. Get a friend to do the action very slowly and to stop at each stage so that you can take a photograph of each small move. Remember to sort the action photographs into the correct order when you get the prints.

Using the zoetrope

Hold the pencil so that the drum is at your eye level. Spin the zoetrope. Look at the photographs through the slits in the drum. Hold the zoetrope carefully so you don't spill the beads.

Don't worry if your photographs overlap a little at the join of the tube. You should still see moving pictures.

The slots are 5.5 cm apart, 0.5 cm wide, and 4 cm deep.

You can decorate the base of the inside of the drum with paper shapes.

BEAD BEARINGS
The beads in the jar lid are not glued in. They are loose so that the drum can spin round on them.

HOW DOES IT WORK?
As each slot in the zoetrope passes in front of your eye, you see each picture for a fraction of a second. Your brain holds one image before the next comes into view, so that the pictures merge. When the drum spins fast, the pictures blend together and seem to move. Cinema film works in the same way.

Decorate the outside of the zoetrope with colourful paper cut-outs.

47

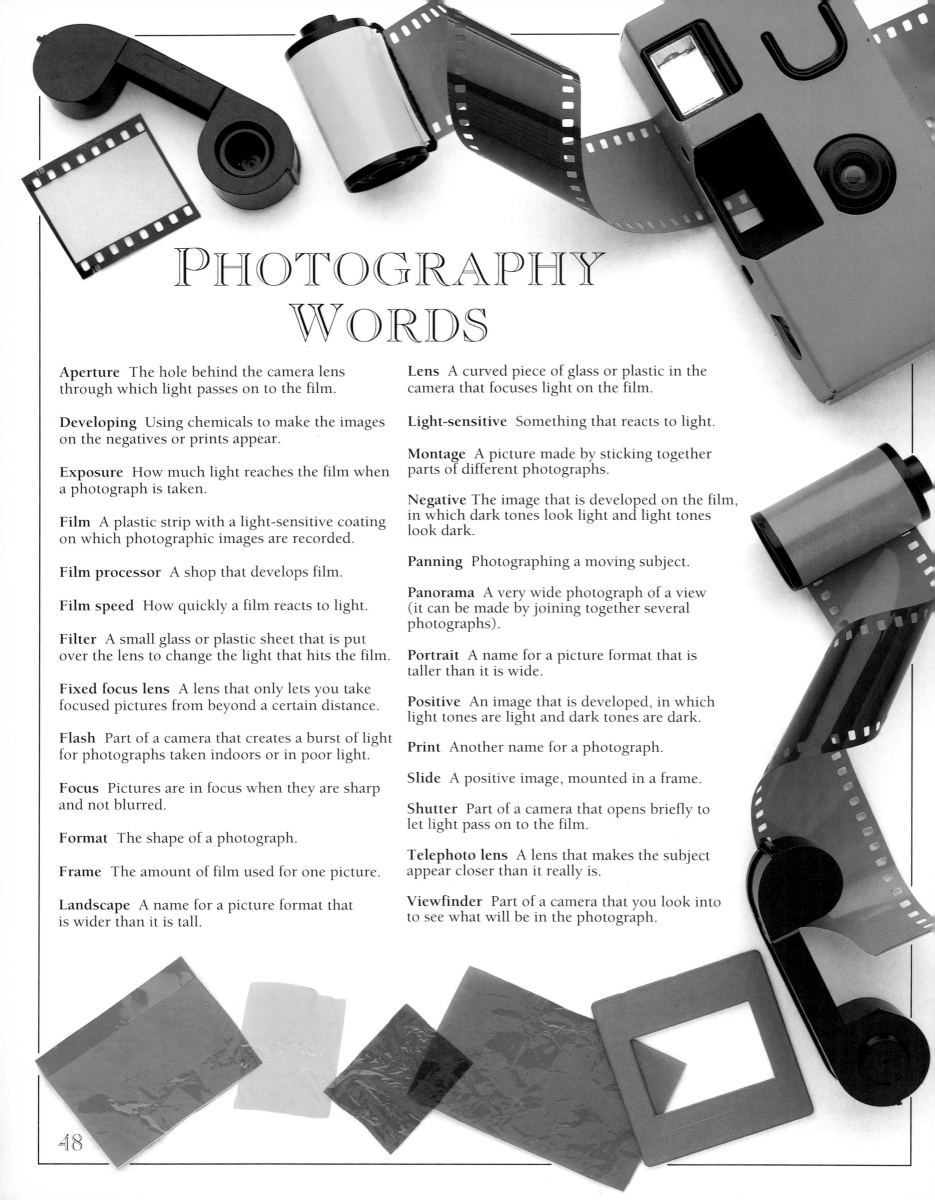

PHOTOGRAPHY WORDS

Aperture The hole behind the camera lens through which light passes on to the film.

Developing Using chemicals to make the images on the negatives or prints appear.

Exposure How much light reaches the film when a photograph is taken.

Film A plastic strip with a light-sensitive coating on which photographic images are recorded.

Film processor A shop that develops film.

Film speed How quickly a film reacts to light.

Filter A small glass or plastic sheet that is put over the lens to change the light that hits the film.

Fixed focus lens A lens that only lets you take focused pictures from beyond a certain distance.

Flash Part of a camera that creates a burst of light for photographs taken indoors or in poor light.

Focus Pictures are in focus when they are sharp and not blurred.

Format The shape of a photograph.

Frame The amount of film used for one picture.

Landscape A name for a picture format that is wider than it is tall.

Lens A curved piece of glass or plastic in the camera that focuses light on the film.

Light-sensitive Something that reacts to light.

Montage A picture made by sticking together parts of different photographs.

Negative The image that is developed on the film, in which dark tones look light and light tones look dark.

Panning Photographing a moving subject.

Panorama A very wide photograph of a view (it can be made by joining together several photographs).

Portrait A name for a picture format that is taller than it is wide.

Positive An image that is developed, in which light tones are light and dark tones are dark.

Print Another name for a photograph.

Slide A positive image, mounted in a frame.

Shutter Part of a camera that opens briefly to let light pass on to the film.

Telephoto lens A lens that makes the subject appear closer than it really is.

Viewfinder Part of a camera that you look into to see what will be in the photograph.